The Other Side of the Fence

Shelly Higgens

authorHOUSE®

AuthorHouse™
1663 Liberty Drive, Suite 200
Bloomington, IN 47403
www.authorhouse.com
Phone: 1-800-839-8640

First published by AuthorHouse 9/9/2009

ISBN: 978-1-4343-8420-1 (sc)

Printed in the United States of America
Bloomington, Indiana

This book is printed on acid-free paper.

Chapter 1

Who decides who their children can be friends with?

LET US START FIRST by saying, that we are not you're normal type of Authors. We are two parents that grew up in middle class neighborhoods, one of us grew up in the City, and the other in the Suburbs. What we can tell you is that never in our lifetime did we ever have to think we would need to deal with Class Opinion Discrimination. The book you are about to read will show you just how kids of today are discriminated against, not for their color or beliefs, but how others perceive their Class distinction. Not through actual facts, but worse yet, by neighbors opinions of the Parents financial position. It is a true story based on true events. We've changed the names to shelter the innocent children that will be forever adversely affected. This is their story...

Chapter 2

Welcome to the neighborhood?

IT ALL BEGAN IN a neighborhood just like any other one. Teddy was four yrs. old at the time and his sister Sally was seven. Houses were just being finished and others were just beginning. Plenty of new friends were arriving almost weekly. Kids of all ages aching to meet their new neighbors. Everyone seemed to be at the same level. Most of the homes were the same style and most families were just starting out. All was well with the world. Hide and seek baseball, street hockey games, basketball, bikes and Barbie's. For the first couple of years, all the neighbors got along and we even attended a Block party. We all loved our new neighborhood. Everyone just about had the same contractor build there house. All the houses were just about the same size and everyone's yard was definitely the same lot size. Mostly all new couples moving in were the same age some had children and others were starting a family also. There were a few older couples who were just looking to settle here to retire. But the one thing that was different about our family was that this wasn't my house, it was my Mom and Dad's house that we were moving into. With my kids (their grandchildren) because unfortunately, I was having some difficult times and was going though a divorce and needed help. I had sold our family house and was unable to afford rent on my own. My family had plenty of room for us, we knew how to make it work, because real families help each other in time of need no matter what. I hated asking for help, but because my children were with me I swallowed my pride and said "I can't do this alone," because my ex-husband decided not to give me any child support I had to take him to court and you know how long that takes.

Chapter 3

Many Friends.

TEDDY AND HIS SISTER played with most of the kids in the neighborhood, but like just about everyone they did have a few favorites that they would become closer to and play with each day for hours and hours. Soon they began to realize that they were a little different than the other kids, they didn't have Dad's. They lived with their grandparents and their single Mom. All of the other kids had both parents. So as time went on questions arose. Other parents would ask Mom if she was married or not? And kids would ask Teddy and Sally " Why do you live with you're grandparents?" It was a difficult time for the kids and Mom and things would only get worse. Mom would always try to brush off the tough questions and tell the neighbors that the marriage just didn't work and they went they're separate ways. Mom didn't feel like it was anyone's business what went on inside our house no one needed to know what mom was going through after all hundreds of people get divorced every day. All families have there own personality problems behind closed doors that they didn't share with anyone why should our family. After all Teddy and Sally acted like all the other children there age why was it okay for people to know that mom was getting divorced but when it was time to ask about anyone else's family it was always hush, hush. Everyone has skeletons in there closet not just Sally and Teddy.

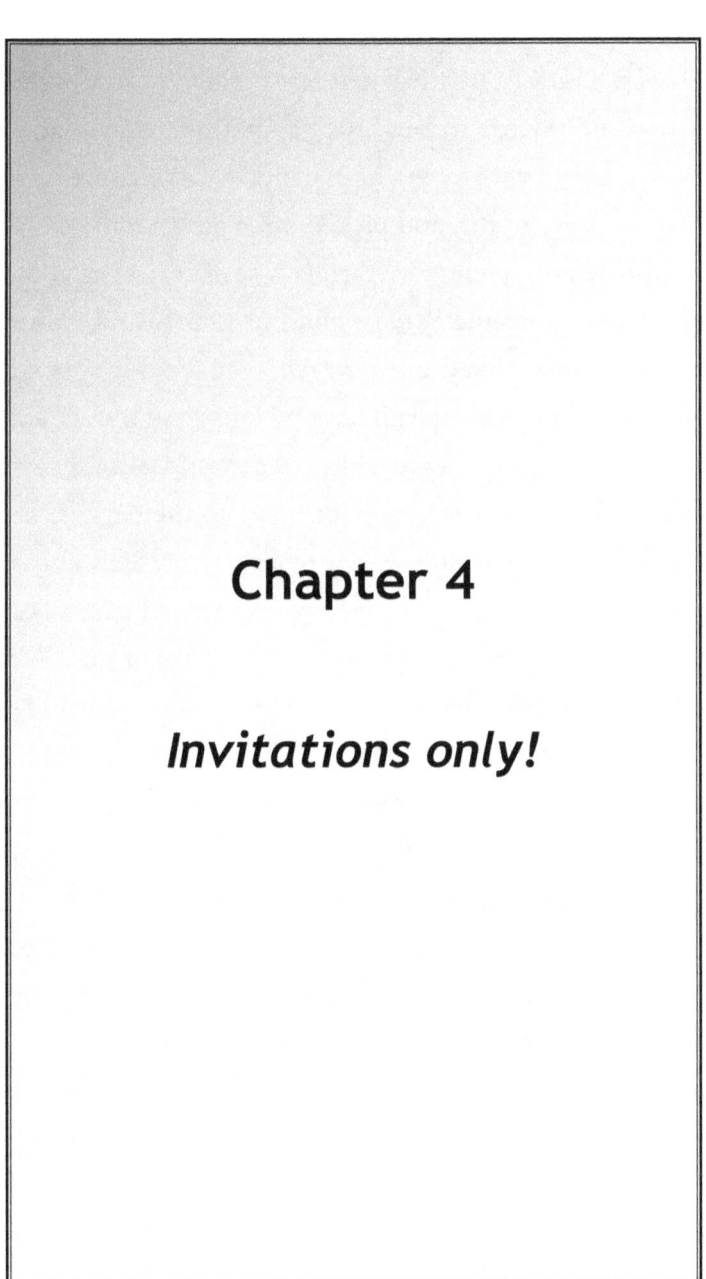

Chapter 4

Invitations only!

THE KIDS FOR THE first few years were always the first to be invited to the birthday parties. They would always attend with a present in hand. We made sure they had on a nice outfit, and picked out a gift that the child would definitely enjoy. We always seemed to get good comments from the Parents and our kids would tell us that they really liked our gift. And, we wouldn't spend a million dollars on the gift, we just made sure it would be appreciated and enjoyable. We would also always offer to bring cupcakes or juice boxes to the party. One other thing, we always would wrap our present, and a store bought card, never would we let them bring a last minute handwritten card or a plastic bagged gift. We also noticed that some Parents, when it was our child's Birthday the Parent of one of the partygoers would give a toy to our son or daughter and also, theirs? Their child would show up with the same gift as they brought ours, and their excuse would be that it was such a fun toy, their child just had to have it also? When Sally & Teddy's birthdays would arrive, the house would be decorated, cake bought and invitations would be sent out. But strangely, no one would come? Everyone had a different excuse, vacations, illnesses, relatives visiting, every excuse they could think up! Even more strange was that We never saw anyone leave on vacation, we never saw anyone's relatives come over and the next day

They all would be knocking at our door to play, even the sick ones? Halloween was always a neighborhood affair, everyone would try to match whatever the hot costumes were for that year. Strangely though the kids would walk together within just a few houses the Stepford wives and husbands would slowly move away from us, it was like a Club that Only MARRIED Parents were allowed to join. We got used to it over time and realized we never wanted an invitation to that Club. We just had fun with the kids. Another Holiday that was a little puzzling was Christmas. Teddy and Sally actually would go out into the neighborhood and sing Carols to the neighbors and deliver Christmas cards and Candy Canes. The neighbors seemed to act like they enjoyed the Holiday Spirit but, as we walked away and the door was closed we would hear them snickering inside as if we were Common Street People. Whatever happened to TRUE Christmas Spirit? We knew then that these people had no Christmas Spirit. They just wanted to know if their new BMW would be under the tree the next morning. That's when we realized that there was much more to this story...

Chapter 5

Keeping up with the Joneses?

SOON AFTER THE NEIGHBORHOOD began changing. If one house purchased a new fence, the other neighbors would have to get a new fence, If one person got a new roof, the other neighbors would get a roof, If one painted their house, the others would paint their's. If one got a new pool, a car, new windows, An addition on their house etc. The contractors made a killing on our block leaving work every day with smiles on their faces. It was like a sick game of follow the leader, but only with grown ups. They were strange about it also; one time we remember when Grandpa offered to help them with one of their projects. They listened to his advice and acted interested but they never took him up on it. It was like they had to hire a Contractor like the neighbor. No way could they ask for help or actually try to save some money, to them that was showing weakness? To us it was saving a little money. Another unspoken rule was your child had to attend Private School if you truly wanted to be accepted by the Inner Circle. We, on the other hand wanted our children to attend Public School as we had growing up. We believe it makes for a well rounded adult. We wanted children, not robots. We also did our own repairs, if there wasn't money than it didn't get done. This was almost comical to watch, because even if they didn't need the same thing done they just had to have it. This is when I began to realize it wasn't based on need it was all about greed! Around the same time I also began to notice that some of the women in our cul-de-sac didn't have to work. They spent most of their days speed walking around the neighborhood, getting their nails done, or just shopping at the Mall. What a life that must be, I on the other hand needed to sleep after working my second job and getting the kids off to school on time. What I did feel sad about, was when I would see them arrive home, no matter how many bags they had, they never looked happy. Theses were definitely Trophy Wives.

Chapter 6

Bra-Burner's (I Think Not!)

WHERE WE LIVED WAS an area of mostly "Stepford Wives." These women would have to leave their house everyday with full makeup on designer clothes hair done etc. If you didn't wear a expensive Business Suit or have a top of the line laptop computer in one hand a leather briefcase in the other, and also an expensive Cell Phone / Fax Machine / Camera / Video Player etc. you were looked down upon. It was so obvious by the look on their faces, that if you weren't properly equipped or prepared for anything possible that you would never fit in. The thing that would always make us chuckle, was that even the wives would leave he house looking like they were going to a Board meeting, when in fact they had nowhere to go except possibly a nail appointment. After School for the Rich kids, was Shopping trips or an expensive dinner. They never would be able to use the Silverware that Mommy & Daddy purchased on Ebay. Another space forward in their twisted game of life was: the tradition when the Husbands would come back from work, they would meet in the driveway, but you never saw a hug or kiss, it was just like a business, not a family. They were just for show. Anyone who went to work and got their hands dirty or wore a uniform was shunned by them. A bad day for us was when we worked a double shift at our second job, We would have to fight just to stay awake on the ride home. Also hoping in the morning we would be alert enough to listen to our kids day or about friends or schoolwork. A bad day for them was a burnt Latte' or a cancelled Hair appointment. None of these women wanted to work, they loved living off their husbands money. Love should be a 50/50 deal, but in their eyes it was 90/10, when it came to helping support the family. Homemaker's my ass! It was more like home freeloaders!

Chapter 7

A day at the Aquarium,
Salon, Supermarket etc.

I CAN REMEMBER ONE TIME like it was yesterday. Our family was on a day trip to the Aquarium. Upon entering We noticed one of the Stepford Wives with their brood of kids and others. When they noticed us, which of course was one of the children (they would have just passed by without saying a word). It was like they were embarrassed to see us outside of our development. The kids tried to stop and say hello, the parents just nodded their head and kept walking so that the kids had to actually run to catch up with them. This is when we knew that outside was even worse. If they had heir friends or relatives with them, all of a sudden we were second class citizens. Another occasion that comes to mind is when I saw one of the Mom's at the Hair Salon. She tried to play the blind mouse. When she actually had to look at me I had to say hello. During this conversation, she would give me nothing but one word answers. I felt as if she was ashamed of me. Another time, at the Supermarket, I noticed one of them in the aisle, and they made eye contact, turned away and went down another aisle. I wasn't expecting a two hour conversation. Just an acknowledgment? But, that is how they were.

Chapter 8

No N.R.A. in our town?

My KIDS LIKED TO play Army, or Cops and Robbers just like everyone in our neighborhoods did growing up. To us, things were so different back when we were young. What was so wrong about admiring a Cop or a Fireman? Or looking up to the people that would protect and serve our community? But a few of our abutters thought differently. They would buy their kids full fatigues and Police / Pirate costumes, but NO Guns!! When our kids brought out their guns to play, the Private School kids would Start to play but constantly have to look over their shoulders for a parent. One time one of the Dad's came over to our house and said " We don't allow our children to play with guns" Grandma said she would respect their rules and that our kids would only play in our yard and the same Dad actually came over another day and had the gall to ask Grandpa if he had any real guns in the house? As if because our kids played with guns, we must have a stash of weapons hidden in our home? Another one of the Super Dads actually bought a Paintball gun for HIMSELF? He would play with it in his yard and make his kids watch him. What a hipocrite! One time we asked him if he ever played guns as a kid, and he just quickly shook his head yes so only we could see, and so his kids wouldn't know the truth. Talking about sending mixed messages, like a kid saying to another kid "Ha,

Ha I can play with this, but you can't! The kids would get upset and ask the Dad, "Why was it O.K. for you to play with guns when you were our age? Of course there would be no explanation. I actually felt bad for the kids. And, strangely enough I would see those same children having a sword fight or shooting a bow and arrow in the yard, and shooting squirt guns at one another. They also seemed to have more than enough violent video games in their homes and that were freely accepted? One time when Teddy went to play with the others, he arrives back fairly quickly. When I asked what had transpired he told me that one Of the Dad's was shooting arrows in the backyard and he needed to go home because he wasn't able to concentrate on his aim with all the neighbor kids watching him. What a joke? To the kids it was just a game, but to the Dad it was like a secret mission in Afghanistan.

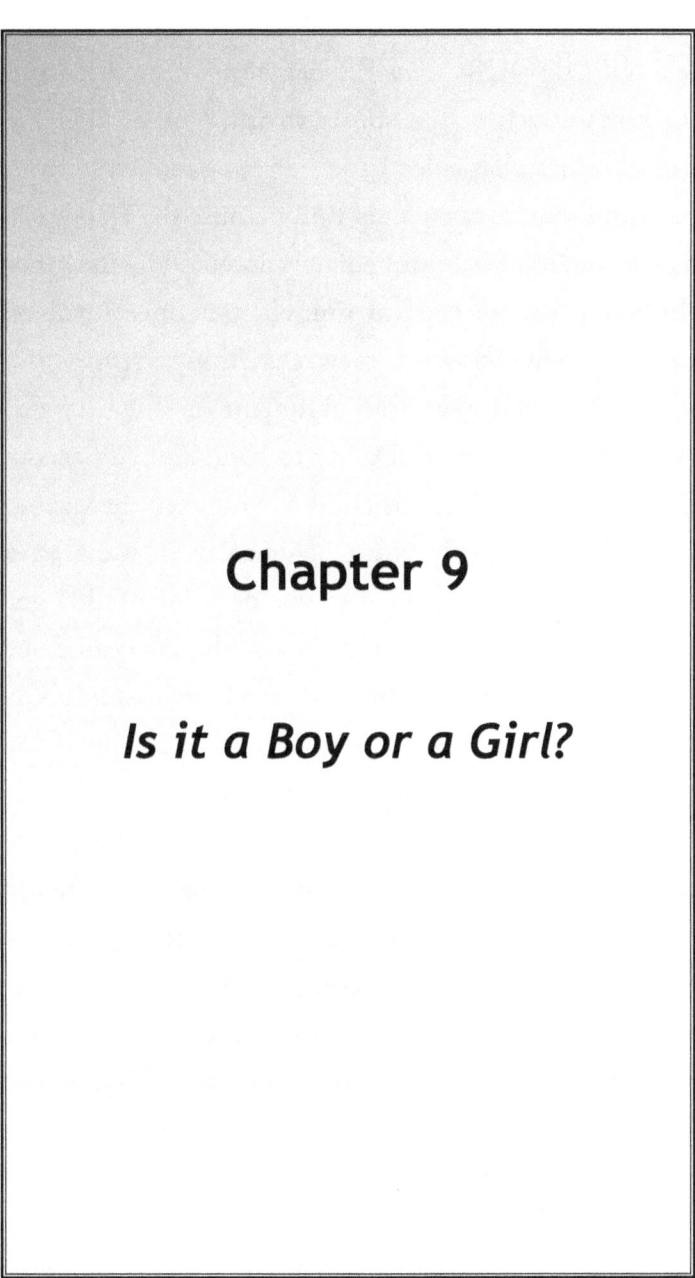

Chapter 9

Is it a Boy or a Girl?

ONE OF OUR NEWER neighbors moved in, and the boy was a little less sporty than the other kids. He would rather play video games or get a manicure from his Mom than play outside. But, because the Dad was a businessman, he was immediately accepted by the inner circle. At first he kept to himself, but once involved with the other kids we knew something wasn't quite right. There was always an argument or situation and he would run home to Daddy to complain. When the Dad would come out, his child was never in the wrong, and neither were the Private School kids. It was always our kid that was at fault. On one occasion, Teddy got into an argument with the child and the Dad came out and had the audacity to not only scold Teddy but point his finger into his chest like he was a bad puppy. If my boyfriend had been home he would have ripped his head off. But as usual he only did it when no one was around. And what made me sick was that while Teddy would stay and take the heat, the Private school kids would run home, and only come out when the situation was over. Then they would thank Teddy for standing up to the kid and say "We hate him too"! And if Teddy told any of the other Stepford Mom's what had transpired they would reply "We don't like to get involved." But what's sad is the very next day, the other Mom's would make their kids play with him even if they didn't want to cause they wouldn't want to break up the "inner circle." So I told Teddy it was better if he just stayed away from that kid, and come home before anything started, and wouldn't you know it, the fights would still go on, but now who could the Dad blame it on?

Chapter 10

Adults can play too...

I FINALLY HAD MET A nice guy who treated both myself and my kids wonderfully. On a few occasions we would actually go in our backyard and play games like: Volleyball, Badmitton, Basketball or Baseball. We would see the other Mom's looking out their "NEW" windows in envy. How sad, they were like prisoners in their beautiful homes. I would almost feel bad for them, even though they could care less about me. The one sport I did see them partake in was power walking the neighborhood ALONE! I would very rarely see them together doing any type of physical activity. I would however every once in awhile see them plant flowers together, but even that was rarity. If our family was outside doing yard work our kids would play by our sides and we would play the radio. One time however one of the Stepford Mom's actually had the audacity to ask us to lower the volume on the radio. This coming from the people that only weeks before had a full blown block party with all the adults getting trashed and lighting off their illegal fireworks. We of course wouldn't be invited, and we would be left to clean up the fireworks in our yard that they would never offer to do. During the parties the parents would be so drunk, they wouldn't even notice kids being nearby swimming alone, jumping on a trampoline in the dark, or walking very closely to the horshoe pit while Horsehoes would fly right past them. I have no idea how they wouldn't get hurt? The part that would make us laugh was when the Upscale Women would go to these parties, they would dress like they were in there 20's. Mini-skirts, American Flag bikinis, Men going shirtless that shouldn't have even done that when they were in their 20's, it was a mess!

Chapter 11

Charity or Farce?

CHRISTMASTIME AND THANKSGIVING DAY always troubled me and my children. We couldn't understand why these husbands and wives would help out the less fortunate and have no problem coming to our door asking for our support which we would. They would even be extremely nice to us that day, but the next day its like we were nothing but strangers in the street. The thing that cracks me up the most is that we all went to the same church, and were taught the same lesson to love thy neighbor as thyself? And no matter what don't judge anyone based on opinion. Did they almost feel good for helping because it was a holiday and they wanted to look good or did they really care? Why go to church and leave not doing what you were taught to? Like loving and helping others out if you can, and don't judge them for any reason.

Chapter 12

Use your OWN Toilet not ours!

YOU'LL LOVE THIS ONE. One day, One of the Moms actually let her child play with mine. Needless to say we were in total shock. They played outside their home for maybe only 20 minutes or so (which was a world record). Sally really needed to go to the bathroom, so she asked if she could use there's. Seeing she was only 8 years old and you know how little kids always have to go . The mother replied, "Sorry Sally, you can't use ours you have to go home and use your own." Sally came running in the house to go. When Sally went back to play the Mother and child had gone into the house. Sally knocked on the door the mother said my child can't play with you anymore today, we're going out later. Sally was never invited over again . What is strange to us is the fact that up until this point, the child was never allowed to play with public school kids ever? This child looked sad outside looking at all the other children play when her Private School friends weren't around. This child could only go to the end of her driveway and no further. She never got her clothes dirty, she was almost like a trained dog. You could see in this child's eyes the sadness. This always broke our hearts.

Chapter 13

Lice or Nice?

ONE AFTERNOON ONE FAMILY in the neighborhood was having a party. Lots of kids to play with, Teddy was actually invited over and he was having fun. They all began to play baseball. Teddy got his glove from home and ran over to play but when it was Teddy's turn to bat, one of the adults told him he needed a helmet for safety. But I remembered that there were plenty of Baseball Helmets for the other kids to share, but why not Teddy? I asked Teddy and he said "I was told they are to small and won't fit me but why did they fit the other children that where older then me?" Strangely as I see, the house he was visiting over had a Father who was a Baseball Coach. He had plenty of equipment around? I think they believed that maybe he had lice or that he sweats differently then the Private School children? Doesn't that make you just want to throw up? Teddy was the best athlete his age in the neighborhood, so we wonder if maybe also the Dad's didn't want him to show up their future Major Leaguers?

Chapter 14

Lets try juggling!

AFTER FIVE YEARS OF living here. My Boyfriend and I decided to start looking for a house to live in. We were so excited to leave this freak show and start fresh. We couldn't take how these kids would love to play with ours one day and then the next day it was like they were on some secret mission and couldn't come out and play. I felt bad, because in our old neighborhood everyone was excepted. I didn't want my kids living in this type of environment anymore. Why did these parent's let there kids play one minute but no the next? That is giving people mixed signals. But because I had been divorced, I was the one that felt responsible for why people treated us differently.

Chapter 15

The new car!!

AFTER WORKING EXTRA HOURS my boyfriend decided to by a new car, his other car was costing too much to fix and it was getting older. After all, we worked very hard and we needed a good reliable car for our family. I worked nights and he didn't like me driving down back roads alone so we needed something new. He looked online and through the auto magazines. Finally he got a really good deal on a real nice car seeing that when he was younger he was a car salesman so he new all the tricks. He bought the car and we all loved it, and appreciated how hard we had worked for it. Every time we all piled in this car, it was like being wealthy for the first time. When I borrowed the car, sometimes I couldn't believe the reaction in the neighborhood. People whom before would have never given me a second glance, were actually waving to me? It felt nice I admit, but I knew they where all a bunch of phonies. When I had my old car the next day and not my boyfriends, I didn't even get a smile or wave. One neighbor was right across from me at a red light, I waved and smiled but received nothing in return? One day as I was driving down my street in my old Jalopie, one of the Stepford Wives was walking down our street it was a beautiful summer day. I went slow by her and I had my window down. I attempted to say hello, and I even called her by name. She looked right at me with a stone cold face, and can you believe she totally ignored me and I never had any kind of run in with her over anything? Another time at the end of our street was a stop sign where someone could wave you on during traffic. This time it was one of the Suits (Men), and he acted like he didn't even see me? What I realized at this point was they weren't saying hello to me or my kids, they were saying hello to our car?? Is that ridiculous or what?? That's how materialistic these people actually had become.

Chapter 16

Moving on Up!

AFTER HAVING JUST ABOUT enough of the judging based on economic conditions. We decided that it was time to escape from our neighborhood prison. We wanted our children to grow up in a different way, without stereotyping. My kids had grown really close to their new Father figure and he treated them like they were his own. So we began our search for the perfect home. It was a long drawn out process with not only qualifying for the mortgage, but also saving for the down payment. We finally were ready to shop. We looked at many houses in many neighborhoods. But there was always an issue. Yard was too small, no parking, busy street, too much work needed, bad area etc. Finally when we had just about given up, we found it! It was everything we dreamed of, a bedroom for everyone, a great big yard and plenty of parking. We made an offer before we could even see the inside, we just knew this was our home. We showed the kids the house and everyone was so excited. The offer was accepted, so we were ready to move in. Family came to help us prepare the house and to paint, clean etc. It took us about a month to have the place ready to live in. Our furniture was delivered, and the new flooring was installed. We rented a Moving Truck and moved from both our places into the new house. We were ecstatic! One thing that we did notice was not one of the neighbors even asked where we were moving, but we shouldn't have been surprised. After settling in to the new home we started to see our kids actually saying hello to all our new neighbors. Everyone seemed to get along wonderfully, and no one was judging anyone else. It didn't matter what car we drove, or what schools our kids attended, nothing was based on material things. It was true friendship. All our new friends came by to welcome us to our new abode. Mr. Squirrel, Mrs. Bird, Mr. Snake, Mr. & Mrs. Rabbit and the kids, and even The Deer family stopped by though they were a little shy. We decided if we wanted true acceptance, we needed to move to the woods. And you know what? We've never been happier or more comfortable. Isn't that sad??